Relationship To Self

A 7-Step Game Plan

To Become Your Own Best Friend

Mario A. Bayne

with

Kathryn Miller Morgan

To
Chico,
& family,

"Best
Hopes
&
Wishes"

Mario

RELATIONSHIP TO SELF
A 7-Step Game Plan To Become Your Own Best Friend

Mario A. Bayne with Kathryn Miller Morgan

Printed in the United States of America

First Printing, January 2011

ISBN# 978-0-9709566-1-3

Published by Eleven Productions, LLC.
P.O. Box 32958
Phoenix, AZ 85064
www.elevenproductionsLLC.com

To order additional books, please contact the publisher at the above address.

Cover design by Kathryn Miller Morgan (www.kathrynmillermorgan.com)

Special thanks to

Blue Cross Blue Shield of Arizona

for its support.

To my heart and soul: my sons, Marques and Corey

We all have within us the power to change lives – whether our own or that of others. Doing so, while staying true to myself and my vision, has been one of the greatest challenges and the greatest gifts of my life.

– Mario A. Bayne

Contents

Forward

I have had the pleasure of knowing Mario Bayne for several years and consider him a friend and inspiration. He has a heart of gold and cares deeply about the success of others, particularly tomorrow's future leaders. The impact that he has made on the lives of youths who would not ordinarily believe in themselves or have the opportunities for success has been nothing short of a miracle. His creation of and commitment to Career Concepts for Youth should be recognized as a masterful approach to bettering lives in a selfless manner.

Mario certainly understands the importance of personal and professional goals. I too value them and believe they need identification well before entering the workforce. We all need to have a strong idea of who we are and where we would like to go in life, but it can be risky when taking failure into consideration.

Most teachers or theorists believe in establishing realistic goals, only those that can be achieved. While I understand and also subscribe to that theory, I pushed myself a bit further. It was always my goal to work for a Major League Baseball team in an executive capacity. Everyone around me would ask, "How will you ever do that when you do not know anyone in the game and there are only 30 teams?" I would also hear, "Be careful shooting for the moon."

While I could appreciate that line of questioning and advice, I also considered it motivational consumption. I say shoot for that moon. If I have my heart and mind set on a desirable goal, nothing should ever stand in my way. Granted, there were several moments along the way when I was forced to question the likelihood of my aspirations coming to fruition.

When I graduated from Arizona State University with a Major League Baseball position in my sights, I had no clear plan or direction and would often become frustrated. Countless solicitation letters went unanswered, while numerous cold call messages went unreturned. Discouraged, yet not ready to surrender, I decided to move back to where I went to high school in order to work for my father and to buy time in search of the answer.

It was during that time that I discovered on television an original graduate school program at Ohio University with the sports administration degree that fed right to the Majors. The program was highly competitive, but I was determined. I was invited to an interview for the elite program, but had no idea that I was one of over 3,000 hoping for acceptance into a class of 25. I performed well and was convinced that I had succeeded, and would now shift my focus as to how I could be the one to earn the only internship from this class with the Los Angeles Dodgers.

Two weeks after returning from my visit, I was shocked to learn that I had been denied admission, and quickly began to wonder whether that moon was out of reach. But I would not turn back. Instead, I elected to attend the annual Winter Meetings for professional baseball in Miami, Florida as part of a career search group.

During one of our group's intermissions, I noticed a sign in the hotel lobby that displayed the special events and meetings taking place there for the day. One read, "Ohio University Alumni Reception at 6pm" – the very school and program that had rejected me just a month prior. Well, I decided to crash that party, spent over an hour telling the director why he had made a mistake, was told to come back for the next year's interviews, was accepted, earned the internship with the Dodgers and have spent over 17 years in this great game.

It would have been extremely difficult to overcome so many obstacles and rejections had I not known and believed in myself. Bayne's attempt to impress the importance of being one's own best friend upon others falls directly in line with my experiences. I was comfortable with myself, clearly understood what I wanted to accomplish, established priorities and values and became my own best friend and main support system. Such a path takes patience and courage, and Bayne's new book will help encourage millions to take such steps.

In a day and age where we parents are hopeful that our children will make proper and responsible choices, this is a must-read for both generations. It frightens and saddens me to see the accessibility to drugs and alcohol, and the public pressures that have destroyed the lives of so many youngsters due to social media and networking. To avoid any cliff falls, our children need to have strength and pride, but most importantly, they must be their own best friends. I want my three children to believe in themselves and have the confidence to make the right decisions.

My oldest son, Logan, did just that a few years back in middle school. He arrived on campus one morning and he and a large group of kids were confronted by a student whose behavior was known to be less than appropriate. The young man pulled a handful of bullets from his jacket pocket and said he would use those with the gun he had hidden in the adjacent park to "take care of" another boy in Logan's class. His plan was to hop the fence at noon, retrieve the pistol and return to campus to take action.

Whether his intentions were real or posturing, Logan knew what he had to do. He quickly ran to the off-duty officer assigned to the campus and shared the story. Some other students had followed Logan to see if he would follow through with his threat of notification, so he knew his decision would certainly not be kept secret for long. By lunchtime, Logan's friends had steered clear of him, while the newly-suspended student's entourage approached Logan and said, "You will be jumped within the next few days." With less than a month to go in the school year, disappointed in the school's lack of disciplinary and security planning for our son's safety, my wife and I removed him from the school and finished that year's education in our home.

Logan was clearly alone that day, detached from the rest of his class and school. But he had chosen wisely and honorably, and we were beaming with pride. He did so, because he knew himself so well and his "best friend" likely agreed with what was right.

I personally thank Mario Bayne for sharing this concept and necessary personal reflection with all of us. Perhaps now, all of my children will make similar decisions. They know my wife and I believe in them, but we will have comfort knowing that they will believe in themselves as well after reading *Relationship to Self – A 7-Step Game Plan to Become Your Own Best Friend*. This book is educational, motivational, inspirational and entertaining, just as its author is. Enjoy!

Derrick M. Hall
President & CEO
Arizona Diamondbacks Baseball

Reflections: From the Author's Sons

There is no one in this world I love more than my best friend! There are a lot of people in this world that I truly care about and would be devastated if I ever lost them – my wife, my family and even my friends mean so much to me. But, without my best friend, I'd be nothing.

See, not only does my best friend understand my values, he also knows my goals – where I started and where I want to end. My best friend understands my abilities and my work ethic. He ensures that when I think of things, I don't think of IF, but rather, I think of HOW, which fuels my drive and work ethic.

Knowing Mario Bayne for all of my life, I'd like to say that I was the poster child for Career Concepts for Youth. Over the 20 plus years that I've spent with CCY, I've learned that self-acceptance is not only powerful, but also vital to everyone's success. Without this, self-worth simply doesn't exist. Without self-worth, drive, determination, ambition, values and goal setting, one cannot reach his or her full potential.

I thank my best friend for allowing me to see the person I want to be, and helping me to work towards our goals every day. I thank CCY, and the vital lessons of Mario Bayne, for teaching me how to set goals and visually validating the meaning of hard work.

Moreover, I thank my dad for introducing me to my best friend – the greatest gift I've received! He allowed me to understand that the person I see in the mirror truly is my best friend. As my best friend holds me accountable to our goals and drives my work ethic, I feel that the sky's the limit and this is a gift I am truly thankful for!

Thanks, Dad!

– *Marques Bayne, August 2010*

Reflections: From the Author's Sons

Having a relationship with oneself is the key to gaining success in life. Through realizing that your true best friend is indeed yourself, you can start to see that you have become stronger. Confidence is key to anything you do. It is important to hold and conduct yourself in a manner that displays your character. By being your own best friend, you truly realize the ins and outs of yourself. You learn to aim high and never settle. What I learned that day with my dad is something I will never forget. By becoming my own best friend, I put myself in the best position to succeed by dreaming and never giving up.

The journey of my father has been a true tale. An immigrant from Panama to the U.S., he grew up in the rough parts of Brooklyn, N.Y. At a young age, he had to learn how to survive on his own with no room for fault. In a place where you either ended up in jail or dead, he surpassed the stereotypical ideas of being a failure. Instead, destiny took my dad another way, far out west to Phoenix, where he established a name for himself. His hard work continues as he now gives the extra push to the Valley's youth – the push he never had.

Life is exactly like a delicious recipe. When you gather the necessary materials to create a scrumptious dish, you will find that hard work is the main ingredient. Good character is the base of the dish – where you start off. You need good character to make smart choices and enable a good heart. Next, make sure to add confidence as it helps the dish grow and mature. Now, throw in a vision to outline a path to create your own success. Once done, add determination and persistence. These spices will help the longevity of the dish to make sure it lasts and never gets old. Finally, mix in some happiness to make sure you have fun along the way. Stepping back to admire the recipe created, you will find that you discovered the CCY curriculum.

– Corey Bayne, Summer 2010

Prologue: Planting the Seeds

I spent almost 19 years in sales and marketing in the hospitality industry, until one day in 1991, fed up and looking for greater purpose in my life, I left the corporate world behind. That same year, I established Career Concepts for Youth.

Career Concepts for Youth is an independent non-profit, partnership between business, industry and civic leaders that encourages young students to stay in school by demonstrating how education can lead to fulfilling careers and lives.

By associating education with jobs that provide excitement, mobility, advancement and public good, school attendance and discipline become more relevant to the student.

CCY's goal is to make each student a partner in our efforts to reduce the dropout rate and increase the education level of the workforce.

It has been a long and sometimes arduous journey from the early days of CCY, but through faith, hard work and a positive mental attitude, we have survived and thrived and are now approaching our 20th anniversary year.

Ten years ago, in my first book, *It's All About Choices For Kids*, I set out to impart that one of the greatest gifts we have in life is the knowledge that we have choices and to be accountable for our own choices.

From *It's All About Choices For Kids*:

> "*Often, when we think of worth we think of value, usually in terms of price. With that in mind, what price can you place on yourself? After all, your personal value, or self-worth, is intangible and is known only to you. Self-worth does not come with a visible price tag, but it certainly does come with a price; one which you cannot see, only feel. As the name implies, self-worth is the value, or worth, that you place on yourself. Self-worth is an agreement between who*

you feel you are and how others see you. It is a critical, fundamental and necessary building block for your development. You can create a sense of innate security by just being yourself. You must develop worth to yourself before you can truly have value to others. Be a best friend to yourself first, then you will be better prepared to be a friend to someone else."

Now, looking toward the 20th anniversary of the CCY program, it is that last sentence from the excerpt above – *be a best friend to yourself first* – that is the essence of what I want to convey to readers in this book.

I believe that everything else in life stems from this one precept. The choices that we make in life – both good and bad – will be informed by our feelings of our own worth and knowledge of ourselves. The level of friendship with oneself will help to determine how well you meet the challenges that lie ahead.

I hope that by helping to plant the seeds of self-worth and self-awareness in our young people today, the future payoff will be a generation of young people who know that they are capable of achieving anything with the right attitude, belief and hard work. It is something that I hope can be engrained in the subconscious of all young people. Self-worth is like armor – a protective covering that belongs to you as you navigate thru life's lessons of preventative action or trial and error

The process of life is about coming to trust yourself more and more. This trust increases our capacity to live in a world of challenges and opportunities. But it all begins with knowing who you are and being a best friend to yourself first.

Mario A. Bayne
September, 2010

Corey's Story

You cannot be lonely if you like the person you're alone with. – Dr. Wayne W. Dyer

One day, I was home early and noticed my son Corey coming home from school looking down and depressed. I met him outside and asked what was wrong. He didn't want to talk about it at first, but after encouraging him, he finally told me that all day at school no one wanted to talk to him. I could see that he was hurt, and while no parent wants to see their child hurting, it was a perfect opportunity to teach a powerful lesson. At that moment, it was very important to make him aware of the value of being his own best friend.

I told him that his primary reason for being at school was to learn. School is not meant to be used as a social club – a hard thing not to do for a sixth-grader. I also explained to him how blessed he was to have a home to come home to, a sibling that took great pride in guiding him and two parents who loved him unconditionally.

Has this ever happened to you? Worrying about what people think or say about you, or feeling hurt by the thoughtless actions of others.

In life, it is okay to be disappointed. But when times become difficult or things don't go your way, always remember: you can spend some quiet time with yourself and be happy by knowing the value of being your own best friend.

It is easy in the world to live after the world's opinion; it is easy in solitude to live after our own; but the great man is he who in the midst of the crowd keeps with perfect sweetness the independence of solitude.
– Ralph Waldo Emerson

It is not enough, though, to be your best friend only when you are alone. As Mr. Emerson said, and as Corey came to learn, you need to carry that relationship with yourself out into "the crowd" – whether you are at school, interacting with your family or participating in team sports, when you are comfortable within yourself, you will find that the actions of others will not bring you down and obstacles in life will not prevent you from reaching your goals.

Inscribed on an ancient Greek temple at Delphi are the words "Know Thyself," and the admonition is as valuable and insightful today as it was in the 4th century BC. It is also a first step in your life journey.

In the following pages, you will learn seven steps to building and maintaining a relationship with yourself:
1. Value
2. Conduct of Acceptance – Attitude
3. Patience
4. Detachment
5. Discipline
6. Knowledge and finally, the ultimate goal,
7. Self-Friendship

These seven steps are the stepping stones toward a better understanding of oneself. They will lead to a strong relationship with yourself, which will allow you to go confidently in the direction of your biggest, boldest dreams. When you have the confidence and drive to achieve, there is no telling where you will go – the sky is the limit!

And it all begins with knowledge of oneself. Becoming your own best friend will not happen overnight, but by beginning to invest in yourself now, the future payback will be tremendous.

"I'm by nature optimistic. Reaching goals isn't for pessimistic people. At all steps of my career, there was someone saying, 'I wouldn't do that. You're too old, too young, too inexperienced.' There are always naysayers. Ask yourself: What is important to me? What is my vision?"
– France Anne Córdova [1]

First Step: Value

A person's worth in this world is estimated according to the value they put on themselves. – Jean De La Bruyere

Always value your spirit as the most special gift that it is. – Mario A. Bayne

The day that my son Corey came home so down and depressed, it was clear to me that he had lost touch with his vision of himself. He was placing value on the actions of others rather than valuing the knowledge of his own special and unique spirit. He had let others make the decision about his worth for him, and suffered a loss in confidence and hurt feelings because of it.

When you learn to have a relationship with yourself – to develop trust and confidence and put forth the effort to define your spirit – you will find comfort in the fact that you know YOU.

What is your vision of yourself…how do you see yourself? Do you value the things that make you uniquely you?

It is important to understand that your vision of yourself adds value to everything you do. How do you see yourself? Are you someone who feels as though they can overcome obstacles, set and meet goals and greet every day like it is a gift? Or do you feel as though the roadblocks in your path are too big to get around, goals are a waste of time and 'why do I have to get up and go to school today?'

If you operate under the first set of values, you are bound to succeed at whatever you put your mind to. Sure, there will be setbacks and days when you don't feel like getting out of bed, but if you place value on each new day being a gift that you do not want to waste, you will be up and ready to take on the challenges that the day brings. If you believe in yourself; if you believe that you can achieve the goals you set for yourself, the battle is half-way fought.

Take the time to sit down and identify the qualities that you value. Then set about obtaining or sharpening them.

Essentially, there are two defining actions in life: Performance and Excuses. Make a decision as to which you will accept for yourself and value that. Then, travel through your day with the understanding of how valuable you are.

> Try this exercise:
> Set a goal for yourself – whether it is a vision of the kind of person you want to be (a great friend) or an accomplishment you want to achieve (100 percent on next week's math quiz).
>
> Then, once a day, say to yourself, "If you think you can, you can. And if you think you can't, you're right."

If you accept the value of performance, you will make time to do your homework and study for the quiz, or you will find yourself showing your friends that you care for them (maybe by helping *them* study for the quiz.) If you put forth the effort, you will most likely meet your goal or become your vision. But, if you make excuses and don't do the work required, you will not reach your goal.

The worth of being positive about oneself cannot be estimated – it is priceless. It is what is in your heart and a part of your spirit; a gift that allows you to never compromise an attitude or your ideals.

> Heart, *n.:* a. the vital center and source of one's being, emotions and sensibilities b. the repository of one's deepest and sincerest feelings and beliefs c. the seat of the intellect or imagination. [2]

What is in your heart? Where do your thoughts lie? Do you focus on your abilities or do you assume disabilities? Where is your daily focus?

Answer these questions and you will be on the road to discovering what you value. Establishing where you place value – what is fundamentally important to you – is the first step in accomplishing your goals. As the saying goes, if you do not know where you are going, how will you get there? If you do not know what you want out of life, how will you achieve it?

Consider the following from *The Dhammapada* – writings of the Buddha.[3]

> *All that we are is the result of what we have thought: it is founded on our thoughts; it is made up of our thoughts.*
> *If a man speaks or acts with an evil thought, pain follows him, as the wheel follows the foot of the ox that draws the carriage.*
> *If a man speaks or acts with a pure thought, happiness follows him, like a shadow that never leaves him.*

Take the time to sit down and really think about those things that you believe in and who and what you place value in. Some of these things may change as you grow and mature, but chances are, the core values that you set down as a young person will stick with you into adulthood.

As you think, you will do, and establishing what you value is crucial to the next step of conducting yourself in acceptance and having a positive attitude.

Game Plan in Action: VALUE

What do you value? It is important to ask and answer this question of yourself throughout your journey toward self-friendship. If you do not know what you value; if you do not know what is important in your life, how will you defend it or achieve it?

For me, I value my family above all – specifically, time with my family and being available for my kids. They are my primary focus and the first consideration in most decisions I have to make.

A few years ago, it felt as though our lives were becoming too fractured and hectic. I had a good job that was mentally challenging and enjoyable, but my values were out of focus. I was constantly rushing to work, rushing home, rushing through dinner, rushing through evening homework, chores, etc.; then, doing it all over again the next day – with no time in between to spend with my kids. My daughter was struggling in school and getting into trouble after school. My son was in daycare and would be starting school the coming fall – what was I supposed to do with him after school? I couldn't very well have him go home with his sister and the after-school programs offered were less than suitable, which was why my daughter simply went home to an empty house. I needed (and wanted) to be home for the kids, but I also needed to work – a dilemma that so many parents face. But because I knew what was most important to me, the decision was simple once I re-focused on my values. When an opportunity to work part-time for a local community newspaper presented itself, I jumped at it. Beyond the fact that I would be able to work from home, I would be working in a field that I loved. I took a cut in pay, but the flexibility that the new position allowed was worth more than any paycheck could offer.

Continued…

Now, five years later, I have gone from a part-time copywriter to managing editor. In addition, I have the time and opportunity to pursue a freelance writing career – something I had always dreamed of doing. And I do it all from a home office where I greet my kids each day as they come home from school.

Our lives are much more settled and the kids are thriving and involved at school. I have been able to spend precious time with them – whether it is attending their club performances or team games or just catching up after a day at school. But if I had not decided years ago what I wanted to achieve and where I placed my value, I may have missed an opportunity to not only be a better mother, but to pursue a lifelong passion.

You cannot achieve what you cannot imagine. So ask yourself, "What do I value?" "Where do I want to go in life?" Stick to those things you value and keep your goals focused in your mind. As Henry David Thoreau said, "I have learned that if one advances confidently in the direction of his dreams, and endeavors to live the life he has imagined, he will meet with a success unexpected in common hours."

– Kathryn Miller Morgan,
Mother of two; freelance writer, newspaper editor

Attitude is a little thing that makes a big difference.
– Winston Churchill

Second Step: Conduct of Acceptance or Attitude

The greatest discovery of our generation is that human beings can alter their lives by altering their state of mind. – William James

Have you ever had something happen that did not go your way? How did you react to that situation? Were you upset, disappointed, angry, negative, happy-go-lucky, did you shrug it off?

Your conduct of acceptance is important. It starts with you accepting yourself.

We all have reacted one way or the other to a situation, person or thing. It is a part of life and it is human to show some type of emotional reaction. But whether you brush yourself off and move on or allow negativity to overwhelm and defeat you is what separates the men from the boys – it is the difference between success and failure.

> *Ninety nine percent of failures come from people who have the habit of making excuses. – George Washington Carver*

Remember, misery loves company. Some friends and peers will try to bring you down. When we react negatively to things that do not go our way, are we seeking approval? Do we have self-doubt?

An example of this in my world of helping kids is reacting negatively when my organization does not receive a grant or an individual changes his or her commitment of support.

It is important after a setback to re-focus your attitude. You need to understand the value to yourself of changing your attitude toward the positive. One way to do this is to recognize the power of gratitude, which means acknowledging all of the things you could and should be thankful for. For instance, plugging in a cord to warm up an iron to iron a shirt – it is a small thing that we may take for granted. But if you recognize how blessed you are to have access to electricity, an iron or even a nice shirt to iron, you will find yourself in a state of gratitude. This, in turn, will help you keep a constant reminder of the big picture – the picture of having a strong relationship with oneself.

Recognize the power you have to change your attitude and move on. You may not be able to control the end result of any given situation, but if you understand it and make the choice of having a positive attitude, it will help you to move on from that moment.

When I was a teenager, I often thought very negatively of myself or blamed myself for not getting what I want, when I wanted it. As a teen, I felt negatively towards myself as I rose in competition in sports. Because of the level of competition, I felt that I was not as competitive skill-wise as I should be. The solution was to practice hard and realize that when the opportunity arose, I could compete at a higher level because I had practiced continually. I had also envisioned myself in that situation and visualized myself succeeding.

Think of a time when you had negative thoughts towards yourself. Examine why you feel this way. Now, turn those negative thoughts into a positive direction or path.

Conduct of acceptance – attitude – is the energy to feed yourself as you build a relationship with yourself.

When you fail in life – and we all fail at some point – a positive attitude will be the key to moving past that failure. Rather than being down on yourself for not making good grades or missing a crucial play, learn from your mistakes and turn the experience into an opportunity to do better next time.

At the same time, when you succeed, a positive attitude will allow you to see what you are doing right and to continue to make the choices that helped you reach your goal, rather than resting on your laurels and no longer seeking further success.

However, there will be times in life when, regardless of making the right choices and being on the right path, events may happen that throw you off track or make a certain goal unattainable. These are the moments when a positive attitude – one of acceptance – will allow you to weather the storm.

Man thinks he lives by virtue of the forces he can control. But in fact, he is governed by power from unrevealed sources; power of which he has no control.

You have heard the sayings: things happen; get over it; the glass is half full or half empty. They are all true. To have a relationship with yourself, you must have a positive mindset.

> Once a day, think about the following: Your mind and spirit are always free for you to use as you wish; they are yours. Use them to your benefit. Never put thoughts in your mind not of a positive nature or of benefit to yourself.

Attitude can be your best friend, or your worst enemy.

Legendary football coach Vince Lombardi said, *"It's not whether you get knocked down, it's whether you get up."*

I remember the feeling of being "knocked down" and feeling helpless. I had a business venture that had failed – time, energy and money was spent with no success. The business venture was gourmet meals in a packet. The manufacturer closed down and I was stuck with thousands of cases of meals and no points of sale – that is, nowhere to sell them. If we sold any, there would be no way of reordering the product.
The first thing I had to realize was that I needed to stop talking to myself negatively; I needed to understand that these things happen. I

had no control over the manufacturer's decision to close its doors – it was done. It was time to learn from the experience and move on. Moving on required me being positive to myself and my surroundings. That is the process of "getting up." So, I decided to donate the product to local food banks and family abuse centers. I felt that, through our failure, we were able to help others benefit.

One of my favorite things to say to keep my attitude right is, *"You can and you will, because you believe you can and you know you will."*

Find a favorite saying to use to keep your mind and spirit strong so that you can continue to grow and have a relationship with yourself

> *I had to make my own living and my own opportunity. But I made it! Don't sit down and wait for the opportunities to come. Get up and make them. – Madam C.J. Walker*

Very simply, you must have a good attitude to build and maintain a relationship with yourself.

Of all of the things you wear, your expression is the most important. You have the ability and are capable of being your own friend. Your values and motivation will determine what you do and your attitude will show how well you do it; practicing patience as you move further toward self-friendship will help you overcome the obstacles in your path.

Game Plan in Action: ATTITUDE

The way a person views something or tends to behave toward something, often in an evaluative way, is attitude. People tend to have a negative or positive attitude toward their tasks. Attitude is the way you present yourself in a particular situation.

Attitude is important because it colors everything you do, say and think. If you have a positive attitude, it is more likely that you will accomplish your goals and overcome setbacks. How you approach a situation or task can predict the outcome of your efforts.

The approach you take may reflect a positive or negative attitude:

1. Approaching a task with a negative attitude often leads to disappointment or an unfinished task.
2. The positive "can do" attitude individual is the type of person who will succeed against all odds.
3. "Do it…no excuse…just effort." This mantra represents the positive attitude needed for success.
4. A person who refuses to accept defeat and is confident of his ability to accomplish a task or solve a problem no matter how great the difficulty, displays a "can do" attitude.

Knowledge and confidence are the key ingredients for developing a positive attitude. Adopting a positive attitude as we go forward in life will yield positive results in our quests.

– Abe Thomas, Architect

Game Plan in Action: ATTITUDE

When I think of the word attitude, the first thing that comes to mind is belief and purpose. While talking this over with a friend, he reminded me of how I literally got to where I am today. In 1993, I decided that I wanted to work in a sports industry. I played college football and thought my interests lay in marrying both sports and business. I *believed* I would be successful, I just needed a chance.

So I sent out resumes to teams and volunteered for a company that assisted professional athletes in the transition from sports to the business world. In doing that volunteer work, I had access to some great people and industry magazines. In one of the magazines I found a job fair/conference that I thought would provide me the opportunity I wanted. I did some research and the conference had some testimonials that sold me. So I took my rent payment for the month of June and spent it on the job fair/conference. I really *believed* that once I got there I could find the opportunity I wanted. The first day of the conference I was overwhelmed with how many great candidates there were at this event. The people there had more education, more experience and seemed to know some of the panelist.

After the first day of listening to the experts on the panels tell the crowd it was about networking and who they knew that helped them gain access and opportunities, I was disappointed. I didn't know anyone in sports and started to think about my rent money. But that night, away from the conference and all of those quality candidates, I decided to change directions and created a unique resume that looked like a sports page.

Continued...

I stayed up all night doing it at a copy store and then in the morning went to the conference to pass it around.

It worked! I got an interview with an NBA team. Just the day before, everyone was talking about a particular opening/opportunity. I never even imagined I could get considered, but the new format gave me confidence. It worked and I sat for one interview and was hired a few days later. I am still working for that organization and I know I owe it all to my attitude.

If I didn't believe I could be successful and I quit, where would I be now? My belief became my purpose and it enabled me to continue to work at finding the opportunity I needed to make it a reality. I truly believe that it is up to me to fail or be successful.

– Chris Montgomery,
Director of premium client services, NBA team

Game Plan in Action: ATTITUDE

Attitude can be defined as the body or manner in which one carries oneself. From this, most would think that attitude is the physical posture of the body that you present to others. But to me, attitude not only consists of the physical exterior presented, but is also composed of a person's mental state. I believe that a person's state of mind plays a large role in what type of attitude that person will portray.

There are several aspects that have led me to this conclusion – one being the death of my mom at such a young age. I lost my mom when I was only 12 years old. Not having grown up with a dad, my mom was everything to me. She put a roof over my head, food on the table, provided me with everything I needed and more.

Continued...

But all of this was taken away in one swift pull of the trigger. Most kids at my age would have lost it; not being able to cope with the fact that the one person you loved unconditionally was gone – taken away from you in the blink of an eye. And most others that could handle that situation would be weak mentally and think that things were owed to them after what they had gone through. But I was determined to not let this devastating event diminish my life.

Soon after this tragedy, I met Mr. Bayne, who would become one of my greatest mentors. I went through his Career concepts for Youth program and from there went on to read his book; *It's All About Choices For Kids.* The book helped me to put things in perspective. It helped me to realize that I had not died with my mom that day and that I still had a long life to live and enjoy. Along with my determination, Mr. Bayne's program helped me to maintain a positive attitude on life and become the person I am. Today, I am a student at Northern Arizona University striving to become an athletic trainer.

– Mykel Bennett, college student

Patience and diligence, like faith, remove mountains. – William Penn

Third Step: Patience

Patience is a bitter plant but it has sweet fruit. – Old proverb

Have patience with all things, but chiefly have patience with yourself. Do not lose courage in considering your own imperfections, but instantly set about remedying them – every day, begin the task anew. – St. Francis de Sales

Patience is a virtue. I am sure you have heard that saying before, but what does it really mean?

Patience is defined as a habit or act of being patient.

Patience is a decision and an ongoing process – being patient when things don't go your way; when you are having a tough time handling your homework; when you are dealing with a friend of family member. How about patience with yourself as you navigate this journey to self-friendship?

It is an exercise. It can be truly difficult sometimes, but the more you practice patience, the easier it becomes and the better the benefits to you.

I remember when I first started Career Concepts for Youth and was trying to recruit businesses, schools and facilitators to be part of the program. I knew that I had to be patient with the process. It was hard to do at times. In the early days of CCY, I had to teach the workshops, find funding, promote and evaluate the results to sponsors and work on fundraising.

I had to keep telling myself to be patient. I had to create thoughts and actions to maintain my patience.

Sigmund Freud said, "Being entirely honest with oneself is a good exercise."

I had to be honest with myself that, if I was going to make this new venture work, it was going to be seriously hard work – no one else would care whether I succeeded or failed. This was something I wanted to do – the bottom line was: it would be up to me. I had to decide whether I really had the strength and stamina and will to make the program a success; and whether I was willing to dig deep and find the additional will to keep moving forward when strength and stamina were waning. But above all, I had to stay strong in the belief in the path that I had chosen and maintain the patience to see it through.

We learn things in our lives through prevention or trial and error. Patience can be a guide as you experience both of these paths.

Think about this for a minute: when you are young, you learn a lot of things are preventable (don't touch the hot oven, you might burn yourself) yet, your curiosity tells you to touch it. After you do, congratulations, you have just learned a lesson via trial and error: you burned yourself.

Is it that life sometimes teaches us and chooses which lesson applies to you at a certain time?

Life always teaches us patience when we do not have time for the lesson. – Unknown

Try being patient in a foreign country where you don't understand the language, or it could be a difficult subject in school that tries your patience. But by trusting yourself – remember your values and positive attitude – you can develop patience as you guide yourself to self-friendship.

The next time that you encounter difficulty being patient, try this exercise – believe me it works:

Just Breathe

Sit up straight. Cover your right nostril with your right thumb and exhale powerfully, then inhale and exhale again. That is one. Do this 10 times. Then, alternate and cover your left nostril with your left thumb, exhale powerfully, then inhale and exhale – 10 times. The result will be calmness and energy.

Breathing is an important tool to use on the road to developing patience and as you work on self-friendship – your relationship with yourself.

It is equally important to understand what impatience means. Being interrupted while you are trying to make a point; when a project you are working on just doesn't seem to be getting anywhere… everything in life, one way or the other, requires waiting and patience. Even in the world we live in with text messaging, e-mail, cell phones, two-ways and instant technology.

Patience is required in a huge part of our life. I remember that every time I take my vehicle in to be serviced. Learn to use it to your advantage and remember to breathe. And when your patience is tested to the extreme, it is time to put into practice the next step in your journey: detachment.

Game Plan in Action: PATIENCE

As I face the stresses and challenges in my life, I seek daily spiritual guidance to help me maintain an inner tranquility. This inner tranquility allows me to practice and incorporate patience when interacting with others. By practicing patience, I am able to be an example to others as I pass through life's storms.

Recently, I had to use patience when informed that, due to budget constraints, a long time sponsorship with a non-profit agency would not be funded in 2010.

After digesting the initial notification, I placed a call to my contact at the agency for a lunch appointment. During lunch, I informed my contact we would not be a sponsor this year. Because of the relationship developed over the years with this agency, we decided on patiently pursuing opportunities for possible sponsorship in 2011.

I also incorporate mental gymnastics in exercising my inner tranquility and not allowing others to take away my Joy.

– Garry Walters, Administrator/Consumer Affairs

He who would be serene and pure needs but one thing: detachment.
– Eckhart Tolle

Fourth Step: Detachment

Do not worry. Try to appear jolly and unconcerned. I have smiled often with the bases full with two strikes and three balls on the batter. This seems to unnerve. – Andrew "Rube" Foster

The definition of detachment is separation; impartiality. It is the ability to step back from a situation – to step away from your emotional involvement in a situation – and see things clearly and objectively. It is the ability to ignore the noise of your detractors and to move in a positive direction toward your goal.

Understand that it does not mean not to care about people or things, just do not allow anything or anyone to sabotage your mission of achieving self-friendship. The difference between success and failure comes down to one thing: your ability to focus on the target. The target is YOU!

Have you ever wanted to do something really badly – perhaps you want to be a member of the cheer squad – but you were unsure about whether you could make it. Maybe someone told you that you are not good enough, so don't even bother to try out. Sometimes people tell us we cannot achieve certain goals because they don't want us to be disappointed. Sometimes people will try to drag you down because they are not able accomplish these things themselves. It is important to learn to ignore this "noise" – to detach yourself from the outside distractions and to move in the direction of your goal. By believing in yourself and working hard on a new dance routine, you may very well make the cheer squad. But even if you don't make the team, by setting a goal and pursuing it, you will have built up the self-confidence to try again next year, or to try another sport or activity.

Detachment helps to keep me focused on my mission to help young people become more self-reliant. Having to be detached from a situation to accomplish a goal is something I experience constantly in my work with youth. To be able to implement my workshops, I rely on grants and corporate commitments. If the commitment falls through and I do not receive the funding needed, I will not be able to provide classroom workshops.

Sometimes, waiting on others to follow through on a commitment timeline irritates me – I sometimes take things personally. I have to remind myself that my goals will be met and that I have to keep going rather than waiting on that individual, and, most importantly, not take the situation personally, as that thought process can lead to being negative.

Accomplishing detachment is important to understand. The attitude of the big picture is critical to understand the power of positive thoughts and action.

Let's say I receive a phone call at my office at 8:30am. It is a sponsor who informs me that they cannot contribute to my organization at this time. I thought that this sponsor was on board and fully supportive of my mission. This is definitely not the desired end result that I had been working on for the last five months.

Since I have a workshop to teach at 10am, it is imperative that I bring closure to this situation. I have to remember the big goal and understand that there might be another opportunity to garner support from them or someone else. I have to keep the big picture in mind and remember that the most important issue at hand is to be prepared and productive in my workshop, which is ultimately the purpose of my organization. Let's say my lesson plan for the day is persistence. What better teaching tool to use than myself in this scenario?

You may get discouraged and have a momentary setback, but the end result is that you must keep going. In spite of situations, especially those beyond your control, detachment is important to the end result.

For example, right before you head out to school, you have a disagreement with a friend or family member. You arrive at school and you can choose to let it linger and affect your entire day, or you can take a moment, detach yourself from that situation and move on – concentrating positively on your day in school.

As my sister always told me, things happen, and this too shall pass.

One tool to assist you in moving forward from a situation is this simple game plan. With it, you can help yourself stay on course and not get thrown off track by distractions or detractors. By knowing and trusting in yourself (self-friendship), you will become stronger and more confident with the effort you put forth.

Four-Step Game Plan to Stay on Course
- Assess the situation
- Create a simple plan
- Take action-direct route
- Evaluate your progress

Imagine being in school and hanging with the wrong crowd. You need to assess the situation – hanging with this crowd could get you in a negative frame of mind where your effort in school is minimal – failing grades, non-respect for yourself and on and on.

Create a simple plan to find a more positive group of friends. Perhaps you could look for a school club that reflects one of your interests, which would allow you to meet new people and occupy your time.

Take action – use a direct route. For example, change your environment by moving away from that negative crowd, hang with the more positive group of people.

By taking action, you can evaluate your progress. How did moving away from a negative crowd and towards a positive one affect your attitude? Did you find that you had more self-respect and were making better life decisions? Did you realize how much the negative people were bringing you down? This is progress. It is important to continue evaluating your progress as you move toward your goal – whatever it may be. This way, you will know if you are on the right path.

Are you willing to make a choice? Do you have the courage to start? Can you make the commitment to finish?

I have always thought of myself as a warrior. According to the *Random House Dictionary*, the term warrior has two meanings. The first literal use refers to "someone engaged or experienced in warfare." The second figurative use refers to "a person who shows or has shown great vigor, courage or aggressiveness, as in politics or athletics." It is also a mentality that is useful in day-to-day matters.

When I first started my nonprofit to help kids, I realized that a fundraiser was important to make people aware of our cause and raise money to implement the programs. I talked to a lot of people regarding a golf tournament, as that type of event is popular and a natural for living in a warm climate. I was told it was not a good idea – too much work; there are over 8,000 charity tournaments a year; I needed to have sponsors, and on and on.

I assessed the situation and realized that, indeed, a tournament with a luncheon or dinner and auction would work if planned correctly. The plan was to start nine months before the event by finding sponsors, a minimum to cover expenses for the event and a small profit before selling golf foursomes. Sponsors needed to be secured and paid three months prior to the tournament.

I took a direct route to action by creating a committee to handle certain aspects of the day: raffle and auction prizes, meals, celebrities, golf course contact, event chairman and foursome sales. We evaluated our progress by meeting monthly until our goals were accomplished.

Two weeks prior to the event, everything was done. We knew that the event was sold out, sponsorships were committed, a menu was selected, an auction host was identified and auction items had been collected and categorized. We knew also how much money we had made from the event. This formula has proven to work – we have done this golf tournament for over 17 years now.

When you see that something is worthwhile, do not be afraid to take it on – be aggressive; be a warrior. Have the courage to set big goals – challenge yourself. It will take stamina (vigor) and you will have to commit to seeing it through, but something worth doing is worth doing with all of your strength. You may feel as though you have waged war, but in the end, win or loose, you will be stronger for having fought for something important.

Ask anyone you respect or look at as a positive role model to tell you how important self-friendship is to having trust, honesty, game plans, confidence, action, beliefs, appreciation and spirit to know who you are and what you want to become. This will happen as you grow, but all of the tools you have at your disposal – your values, a positive attitude, patience and detachment – will be useless if you do not discipline yourself to use them properly.

Game Plan in Action: DETACHMENT

Are your feelings hurt when people say or do something that upsets you? Can one unpleasant person ruin a perfectly good day? The ups and downs of daily events can disturb us, disrupt our focus and stop us from enjoying life. One good way to avoid the suffering is to learn a little detachment. Separating or disconnecting from those unavoidable external circumstances means not allowing a situation to dictate our day.

Once we learn to keep our cool and not allow people or circumstances to push our hot buttons, we are able to stay in a peaceful place and not "sweat the small stuff." And let's face it – most of our daily drama is small stuff. Remember that the only person that controls you is *you.*

Detachment is not indifference. If you choose to observe and not react, you'll learn not to take things personally and calmly accept whatever circumstances come you way.

Katherine Koenig, Journalist

Have a vision. Be demanding. – Colin Powell

Fifth Step: Discipline

*Self-respect is the root of discipline: the sense of dignity grows
with the ability to say no to oneself. – Abraham J. Heschel*

Discipline is an ongoing, never-ending mindset.

Sounds simple – it is not really. Most human beings at some point
show a lack of discipline, and for so many reasons. Let me share an
experience I had with a student in one of my workshops years ago.
On that particular day, I was discussing the topic of discipline with a
group of about 35 sixth-graders when a student said to me that being
disciplined was hard and uncomfortable.

I simply told the student, "Discipline is a choice."

Discipline in discomfort can actually become a state of comfort in
that it forces you to see the big picture, to set goals, to be focused, to
exhibit persistence, to be determined – from this you will achieve a
sense of accomplishment. In sports, it means the pain and sacrifice
to get in peak physical and mental conditioning; to become better
through practice and repetition – to give your best effort regardless
of the outcome. For young people, it means to apply all of the above
in their journey to self-friendship.

Comfort is like relaxing; it is a pattern or a habit. Discipline is
learning, trusting and unleashing commitment. Commitment, in turn,
separates doers from dreamers. Commitment starts in the heart; is
tested by action; then opens the door to achievement.

In my conversations with a variety of people, I have found that there
are basically four types of effort people exhibit – young, old, boy or
girl:

1. Cop-outs: people who do not have goals and do not commit

2. Hold-outs: people who don't know if they can reach their goals, so they are afraid to commit.
3. Drop-outs: people who start toward a goal, but quit when the going gets tough.
4. All-outs: People, who set goals, commit to them and pay the price to reach them.

Train yourself to make good use of your time. Have fun with yourself. Study yourself and identify your strengths – then build on them. You will invest your life in something or you will throw it away on nothing.

Discontent is want of self-discipline; it is infirmity of will.
– Ralph Waldo Emerson

Think about this for a minute, do you want:

- **A lifestyle of giving up?**
- **A wrong belief that life should be easy?**
- **A wrong feeling that success is just being lucky?**
- **An attitude of negative thinking?**
- **An acceptance of other people's fences?**
- **An irrational fear of failure?**
- **A lack of vision?**

One half of knowing what you want is the knowledge of what you must give up before you get it. Nobody who ever gave his or her best regretted it. Understand that to develop commitment to discipline has nothing to do with talent or ability. It has to do with work. Never accept the negative until you have completely and thoroughly explored the positive.

"We all have dreams. But in order to make dreams into reality, it takes an awful lot of determination, dedication, self-discipline, and effort." – Jesse Owens

Be disciplined with yourself and find out.

Game Plan in Action: DISCIPLINE

Discipline…to most it elicits an emotion of pain, discomfort or having to do something difficult. It's a word we like to avoid; it's just too much work. Discipline to me, however, means the exact opposite – it's been the most important tool to my success. Discipline equals results, and even better, predictable results. If I do something with discipline, I get the same result each time. For example: When I exercise I feel better, when I eat healthy I feel good and when I do these things consistently with discipline, I get results – consistent, predictable results.

The same has been true in my career and passion as a chiropractor. When I first started out, I lived, ate and breathed chiropractic, learning everything I possibly could. Through this process, I quickly learned that using a system and being disciplined about following these systems produced results – consistent results. If you are disciplined enough to grow and learn it will result in success, it has definitely given me the drive to succeed in my life and my business.

As a chiropractor, the greatest discipline for me is to be "present-time conscious." What does that mean, you ask? It means that I have to be both physically and mentally present. It is the core principal to being a successful chiropractor. I have to be present with the patient, regardless of anything else that is going on in my office, my personal life or even my own body.

Continued…

At that moment, it is all about the patient, I must give them my undivided attention. And with each patient, throughout the day, I must stay both physically and mentally present. With so many distractions in life at any given moment, it takes a strong, disciplined mind to stay totally focused on the patient. It's the quality, not the quantity, of the time spent with each patient that comes in to my office that makes the difference. Being physically present and mentally absent will not result in success. The discipline of being present-time conscious is what separates the successful chiropractor from the rest. The past is over, the future hasn't happened and all we have is right now.

– Dr. Michael Cormier, Chiropractic physician

When I discover who I am, I'll be free. – Ralph Ellison

Sixth Step: Knowledge

Knowing others is wisdom, knowing yourself is enlightenment.
– Lao Tzu

Knowledge is defined in the dictionary as understanding gained by experience; range of information.

Who are you? Have you ever asked yourself that question?

Someone once told me that the single-most important ingredient in the formula of success is to know how to get along with yourself and other people.

I'll share something with you that I experienced years ago when I was a counselor for a youth sports program. One day, four of the youth participants said to me that I was a very good athlete in my day. They wanted to know if I could dunk a basketball.

I said, "Sure, but I won't do it for free."

So, they pooled their money together and it came out to $8.34. I, of course, was joking with them. I said I was not warmed up and I had other things to do when one young male said, "You are making excuses."

A young female then said, "You are always telling us, 'no excuses, just try your best.'"

I thought to myself, "You have to try." And as I ran toward the basket, I knew I really had to make the dunk. As I lifted off my left leg, I heard something pop in my knee. I knew that familiar sound. It was one that I had experienced before; one that had ended my once promising athletic career.

I made the dunk, but as I landed, I felt this needle of pain inside of my left knee. By the time I arrived home, my knee has swollen tremendously. By the way, I did take the $8.34 that the kids had offered. They said I deserved it.

After two days, my knee was not getting any better. I went to see my doctor, who sent me to a knee specialist. They took an MRI – an x-ray of the inside of my knee. I had torn the cartilage and damaged the knee – the same knee I had hurt before.

I was so upset with myself for allowing someone to challenge me to prove a point. I will never forget this moment – I kept a copy of the doctor's report and wrote something that I always use to remind me of the importance of knowledge:

"Good judgment comes from experience and experience comes from bad judgment."

The experience reminded me that I needed to trust my own judgment. Remember that it is your actions and attitude when you are on your own that reflect who and what you really are. When you are working on being the best you can be and you know who and what you really are, you are able to carry that knowledge with you every day. It will help inform your judgment as you interact with others. This self-knowledge will help guide you to self-confidence, which in turn allows you to trust in yourself.

The process of life is about coming to trust yourself more and more. Trust increases our capacity to live in a world of challenges and opportunities.

Knowledge is power. – Sir Francis Bacon

One important factor to consider in your journey toward self-knowledge is the knowledge of your elders – knowledge that comes from experience. Your parents, grandparents, aunts, uncles, educators and coaches have a lot to teach you – but you need to be open and responsive to their instruction.

You may feel as though your parents are "out of touch" or just "don't get it," but, believe me, they have been there, done that and have the T-shirt to prove it. Some lessons in life, we have to learn on our own…sometimes the hard way. But the elders in your life – those who care for you and look out for you – can help guide you toward self-knowledge and successfully into adulthood.

> *If a person refuses to learn, then he is only hurting himself. But the person who listens when someone tells him he is wrong will understand more and more. – Proverb*

What you may see as restrictions by authority figures are actually precautions set in place by those who have been there before you. When a parent says something like, "don't play with matches," or when they set a curfew, it is for your own safety and to instill the value of responsibility.

As you grow and mature, especially moving into the teen years, be very wary of relying solely on your own advice – you are, in many cases, treading in brand new territory. Look to those who have been there before you. You may feel that your parents don't understand you, and they very well may not "get" the latest clothing fad or see the attraction of the various online communities you frequent – but the core experiences have not changed much from the time when they were young. The technology has advanced and the pace of life has increased, but the human experience is much the same.

Beyond learning from those elders immediately in your life, it is also important to be well-read. Good books can expand your mind and open up new horizons – showing you the boundless possibilities of the world around you. Take advantage of your school and public library. They hold such a wealth of information and knowledge – knowledge that will help fill the crucial gap between learning and doing. The best way to be prepared for life's events is through obtaining as much knowledge as you can, then implementing what you have learned when the time comes. Knowledge truly is power.

You will find in life that you never stop learning. There are always new life lessons popping up; always new technology; always new ways of doing things. Stay informed and keep your mind sharp and active – there is always room for improvement and looking for knowledge and wisdom wherever it can be found is important.

Remember on this journey toward self-friendship, that your job is to constantly nurture within yourself the characteristics of knowing your value, conducting yourself in acceptance with a positive attitude, patience, detachment, discipline and knowledge.

Learn to be a best friend to yourself: allow yourself to be you, and always let your best shine through.

Game Plan in Action: KNOWLEDGE

The word knowledge is a noun that has multiple meanings as well as uses. Derived from the word know, knowledge is often associated with a particular context in mind. Do you know; did you know; and what do you know? Knowledge is wisdom, learning, awareness, enlightenment, information, knowing, understanding, intelligence and power. However, knowledge without action is not power. Knowledge is the sum of what is known.

As an educator, I am quickly drawn to defining knowledge as an acquired understanding of learning. It is well documented that one of the best teachers is repetition, and with repetition one acquires a keen sense of what is known.

Continued…

You acquire a deeper understanding of why you know what you know.

Throughout one's journey, which can include a combination of education and travel, relationships and cultural exchanges, one acquires a certain expertise on the how and the why. One becomes suspended in a state of knowing. You become familiar with a subject of learning. So to me, knowledge has always been about at first learning, then about teaching.

– Wiley Davis, Educator and Coach

My best friend is the one who brings out the best in me.
– Henry Ford

Seventh Step: Self-Friendship

"One of the greatest things you have in life is that no one has the authority to tell you what you want to be. You're the one who'll decide what you want to be. Respect yourself and respect the integrity of others as well. The greatest thing you have is your self-image, a positive opinion of yourself. You must never let anyone take it from you." – Jaime Escalante

Through the years – by putting into practice the principles of value, conduct of acceptance, patience, detachment, discipline and knowledge – my son Corey has grown to learn about and to understand himself. With this development, he has become "Mr. Popularity." Gone are the days of hurt and loneliness at school, in large part due to his spirit, his clear self-friendship and his soul. We often joke and say that he has an old soul.

How do I see myself? Ever ask yourself that question, whether things in your life are going good or bad?

Sometimes when things are going bad, you see yourself in a bad way. For example, getting your report card and finding out that you have some failing grades and that you did not really put the effort in your work that would have resulted in a passing grade. Perhaps you were not concentrating, were talking in class or were lazy about your homework – believe me, I have done it.

It is your actions and attitude when you are on your own that reflect what and who you really are.

You could make a better effort to study, not get distracted in class by talking too much and get a study partner to do your homework with.

You see, if you beat yourself up after the fact, you have accomplished nothing. Be a friend to yourself and accept the fact that you ultimately are responsible for your failing grade. Then, make the effort to correct it.

Understand that nothing is more difficult to accomplish than changing outward actions without changing inward feelings. Think about it, whose life is this anyway? What is best for you?

In my workshops with young people, I am aware of how this trait is lacking. You must understand the importance and effort it takes to be your own best friend.

Try this exercise the next time you want to feel better after your efforts result in a negative situation:

> Accept the situation for what it is and move on. Remember, the relationship is for you and about you.

In his poem *Self-Reliance*, Ralph Waldo Emerson says, *"What I must do is all that concerns me, not what people think."*

Here is an example: imagine that you are working on a big project that you need to complete over the weekend – the teacher will not accept it late. This is no ordinary project, it is one that you want to do a really great job on – the year so far has not been the best and you want to prove to yourself that you can make this the best project in the history of projects. Besides, the topic of the project is one that you really love, so it has extra meaning to you.
But, the big blockbuster movie that you have been waiting for opens this same weekend. All of your friends are going and they are trying to get you to go as well. While you really want to share the experience of seeing this movie with your friends, you have made your class project your number one priority. When you tell your friends that you can't go because you really want to do a good job on your project, they laugh and say you are such a nerd to want to do so well on a dumb class project. They say that you won't get the

opportunity to go with them to see the big movie again – the class project may not be your best, but it is "good enough" to turn in. You have set a goal for yourself. It is important to you – one that you hold great value in. But you won't have the opportunity to see this particular movie with all of your friends on opening weekend again. So you have a choice to make: do you stand firm in your desire to meet your personal goal and do your personal best; or do you compromise the value that you have placed on your class project and, not wanting to be thought a "nerd," place more value in what your friends are saying to you.

Life is full of challenges and choices. Sometimes the choices we make do not have the outcome we would have wanted. But the more you allow yourself to compromise what you believe in – by letting others sway you from your goal – the more you chip away at your own self-worth. When you stand firm in your choice, not only will you respect yourself more, your friends will recognize and value this strength in you as well. By being your own best friend first, you will be a better friend to others.

Game Plan in Action: SELF-FRIENDSHIP

The word self-friendship carries substantial meaning for me. I think of the journey I have traveled, and continue to travel toward the goal of self-friendship. It has taken me some time to realize that I cannot wait for the rare occasions when I am on vacation or when I can be alone without children, grand children running around or the distractions of TV and radio, the normal sounds of a household or not involved in a meeting with colleagues at work. I have learned to stop periodically – sometimes in the midst of whatever chaos is going on in my life at the moment, sometimes only for 10 minutes if that much – close the door to my bedroom or to my office and just still my thoughts and focus on my relationship to myself and to my God. I listen and focus on my breath and mainly I give thanks for health, for strength; for all the many blessings in my life, despite the circumstances being faced at the moment. I tell myself positive and loving thoughts, without being egotistical, selfish or self-serving. In other words, I try to get along with myself, because even if we move to another state, country or the moon, we cannot get away from ourselves. So rather than wait for my circumstances, environment, finances and the people in my life to change, I try right where I am every day to get along with myself; to be a friend to be myself; and in that process to get along with and be a friend to those around me. Therein lies inner peace, true friendship with self and others and ultimately, lasting happiness.

– Dr. Marcia Bayne Smith, PhD, Sociology

The Payback

Success is to be measured not so much by the position that one has reached in life as by the obstacles that he has overcome while trying to succeed. – Booker T. Washington

In this book, I have set out to help you understand how to achieve friendship with oneself. Being your own best friend is an investment in your future. As I stated at the beginning, becoming your own best friend will not happen overnight, but by investing in yourself now, the future payback will be tremendous.

Pay·back *n.* A benefit gained as the result of a previous action. [4]

When you are able to identify and Value the amazing qualities you possess; learn to Conduct yourself within Acceptance, with a positive Attitude; practice Patience as you work toward your goals, always moving ahead with Discipline and a sense of Detachment from the negative noise around you; you will be comfortable in the Knowledge that you have created Self-Friendship. This friendship will guide you through the rest of your life.

With every step along your current path, you are moving closer and further toward your future. What will you make of it? Who is it that you want to become? What is it that you want to achieve? You may not have all of those answers now, but I hope that I have given you the tools to set about answering those questions and reaching your desired destination.

Know that within every situation there are choices and once you decide what you want for yourself, create a game plan and work responsibly towards obtaining that goal. It requires effort, and the power of accepting ourselves while following our dreams, knowing that the best way to predict your future is to create it.

Imagine looking in a mirror, and that mirror shows not only who you are, but where you are in your life…and what it took to get there.

William Shakespeare wrote, *"…and since you know you cannot see yourself so well as by Reflection, I, your glass, will modestly discover to yourself that of yourself, which you yet know not of."*

If you are failing a particular class in school, being told you are lazy or don't care about your life or are giving up too easily, it may be time to reassess your values. By working hard with belief, acceptance, a positive attitude, and strong discipline, with a sense of detachment from negative influences, you will find the knowledge you need to make the needed changes in your life. By applying a positive Game Plan to your life, you will soon be passing that class and proving to yourself that your detractors are wrong. You will find yourself setting goals and achieving them. Through your efforts, you will discover who you are and just how much you are capable of. That is what having a relationship with self is about.

A legendary college basketball coach once said that things turn out the best for the people who make the best of the way things turn out. This is the attitude behind the old saying "turning lemons into lemonade." Take the potentially sour events that happen in life and make something sweet out of it. Turn every obstacle into an opportunity to achieve and overcome and transform every negative into a positive growth and learning experience.

Make the most of every day! Each day is a gift and holds endless opportunity. The key is to take what you learn – from your own experiences of trial and error or from the experiences of others – and to apply it positively to your current situation. This will allow you to continue to grow in your relationship with yourself, which, in turn, will allow you to grow and thrive in your relationships with others in your life.

A few final thoughts:
The journey towards knowing oneself better never ends. When you think that you have all of the answers, you don't.

Begin every day by giving thanks. Stay in gratitude, always moving forward, toward your vision.

It is important to know that IT will happen. Believe, then, let it go. Act like it is done.

And remember to breathe and understand that it is never, ever too late to have a strong, healthy friendship with yourself – your best friend.

All the knowledge I possess everyone else can acquire, but my heart is all my own. – Johann Wolfgang von Goethe

---

Expand Your Knowledge: Who's Who of Quotes

Throughout *Relationship to Self,* we have included quotes from a number of remarkable individuals. Whether sports heroes, writers, entrepreneurs, spiritual leaders or heads of state; their words of wisdom can help inspire you in your own journey toward self-friendship.

Below is a brief introduction to each individual – allow their collected words to encourage you and their individual life stories to motivate you.

Page 3   **Dr. Wayne W. Dyer** – *American self-help advocate, author and lecturer.*

Page 3, 27   **Ralph Waldo Emerson** – *(1803-1882); American philosopher, lecturer, essayist and poet. He is best remembered for leading the Transcendentalist movement of the mid-19th century. He was seen as a champion of individualism.*

Page 5   **France Anne Córdova** – *American astrophysicist, researcher and university administrator. She is the 11th president of Purdue University.*

Page 6   **Jean De La Bruyere** – *(1645-1696); French essayist and moralist.*

Page 9   **Winston Churchill** – *(1874-1965); British politician and statesman known for his leadership of the United Kingdom during the Second World War. He served as prime minister from 1940 to 1945 and again from 1951 to 1955 and was also a noted orator and historian.*

Page 10   **William James** – *(1842-1910); Pioneering American psychologist and philosopher who was trained as a medical doctor. He was the brother of novelist Henry James and of diarist Alice James.*

Page 10   **George Washington Carver** – *(1864-1943); American scientist, botanist, educator and inventor. The exact day and year of his birth are unknown but he is believed to have been born before slavery was abolished in Missouri in January 1864*

Page 13   **Madam C.J. Walker** – *(1867- 1919); African American business woman, hair care entrepreneur and philanthropist. She made her fortune by developing and marketing a hugely successful line of beauty and hair products for black women under the company she founded, Madam C.J. Walker Manufacturing Company.* The Guinness Book of Records *cites Walker as the first woman who became a millionaire by her own achievements.*

Page 16   William Penn – *(1644-1718); English real estate entrepreneur, philosopher and founder of the Province of Pennsylvania, the English North American colony and the future U. S. state of Pennsylvania. Under his direction, the city of Philadelphia was planned and developed.*

Page 17   St. Francis de Sales – *(1567-1622); Bishop of Geneva and a Roman Catholic saint.*

Page 20   Eckhart Tolle – *German-born writer, public speaker and spiritual teacher. He is the author of the bestsellers* The Power of Now *and* A New Earth.

Page 21   Andrew "Rube" Foster – *(1879- 1930); American baseball player and manager and the founder of the Negro Leagues. He was elected to the Baseball Hall of Fame in 1981.*

Page 25   Colin Powell – *American statesman and a retired four-star general in the United States Army. He was the 65th United States Secretary of State (2001–2005) and the first African American appointed to that position. He was also the first, and so far the only, African American to serve on the Joint Chiefs of Staff (1989–1993).*

Page 26   Abraham J. Heschel – *(1907-1972); Warsaw-born American rabbi and one of the leading Jewish theologians and Jewish philosophers of the 20th century.*

Page 28   Jesse Owens – *(1913-1980); American track and field athlete. He participated in the 1936 Summer Olympics in Berlin, Germany, where he achieved international fame by winning four gold medals: one each in the 100 meters, the 200 meters, the long jump and as part of the 4x100 meter relay team.*

Page 29   Ralph Ellison – *(1914-1994); Novelist, literary critic, scholar and writer, Ellison is best known for his novel* Invisible Man.

Page 30   Laozi – *(Also Lao Tzu and other variations); Philosopher of ancient China, and a central figure in Taoism. Laozi literally means "old master." According to Chinese tradition, Laozi lived in the 6th century BC and is traditionally regarded as the author of the* Tao Te Ching.

Page 31   Sir Francis Bacon – *(1561- 1626); English philosopher, statesman, scientist, lawyer, jurist and author. He is known as the Father of Empiricism and his scientific dedication probably led to his death,* *so bringing him into a rare historical group of scientists who were killed by their own experiments.*

Page 34   **Henry Ford** – *(1863-1947); Prominent American industrialist, supporter of workers' welfare and pacifism, the founder of the Ford Motor Company and father of modern assembly lines used in mass production. His introduction of the Model T automobile revolutionized transportation and American industry.*

Page 35   **Jaime Escalante** – (*1930- 2010; Bolivian-born American educator well-known for teaching students calculus from 1974 to 1991 at Garfield High School, East Los Angeles, California. Escalante was the subject of the 1988 film* Stand and Deliver.

Page 38   **Booker T. Washington** – *(1856- 1915); American educator, author, orator and political leader. He was the dominant figure in the African American community in the United States from 1890 to 1915, and was representative of the last generation of black leaders born in slavery and spoke on behalf of blacks living in the South.*

Page 40   **Johann Wolfgang von Goethe** – *(1749- 1832); German writer and polymath (Renaissance man). Goethe is considered by many to be the most important writer in the German language and one of the most important thinkers in Western culture. Goethe's works range from poetry, drama and literature to theology, philosophy and science; his magnum opus is the two-part drama* Faust.

SOURCE: All biography information courtesy of www.en.wikipedia.org.

Bibliography

1. France Anne Córdova quote appeared in a 1996 article in *The Hispanic Outlook in Higher Education*. Source: www.womenshistory.about.com.

2. Definition of "Heart" courtesy of www.thefreedictionary.com.

3. The English translation of *The Dhammapada* is by Friedrich Max Müller (1881). Source: en.wikipedia.org/wiki/Dhammapada

4. Definition of "Payback" courtesy of www.thefreedictionary.com.

About the Author

Mario A. Bayne takes great pride in his work with children as the founder and president of the non-profit organization Career Concepts for Youth. A natural affinity exists between Mr. Bayne and the young people he mentors, due to the ease with which he establishes rapport by communicating powerfully from the heart. In June 2011, CCY celebrates 20 years of helping young people.

Some of his other affiliations include Parent and Community Involvement Planning Committee member for the State of Arizona Department of Education; Board of Directors Executive Committee, secretary for March of Dimes Arizona; Phoenix Youth and Education Commission; Phoenix Suns Charities; and chair for Valley Youth Leadership Selection Committee.

In 1991, CCY was awarded the Hispanic Chamber of Commerce Small Business Administration "New Business of the Year" Award. In 1996, Mario was the recipient of the "Friend of Phoenix" Award. Mario is a member of the *Arizona Republic* Parent's Advisory Panel and a board member of the Phoenix Suns Sixth Man Advisory Board.

Mr. Bayne resides in Phoenix, Arizona.